AMERICAN DUENDE

JAY GRISWOLD

DOS MADRES

2025

DOS MADRES PRESS INC.
P.O. Box 294, Loveland, Ohio 45140
www.dosmadres.com   editor@dosmadres.com

Dos Madres is dedicated to the belief that the small press is essential to the vitality of contemporary literature as a carrier of the new voice, as well as the older, sometimes forgotten voices of the past. And in an ever more virtual world, to the creation of fine books pleasing to the eye and hand.

Dos Madres is named in honor of Vera Murphy and Libbie Hughes, the "Dos Madres" whose contributions have made this press possible.

Dos Madres Press, Inc. is an Ohio Not For Profit Corporation and a 501 (c) (3) qualified public charity. Contributions are tax deductible.

Executive Editor: Robert J. Murphy

Illustration & Book Design: Elizabeth H. Murphy
www.illusionstudios.net

Typeset in Adobe Garamond Pro & Iowan Old Style
ISBN 978-1-962847-31-5
Library of Congress Control Number: 2025942575

ACKNOWLEDGEMENTS

'An Introduction To The Alphabet': *5 AM*

'The Tunnel Rat': *Negative Capability*

'The Veteran,' 'Funeral Procession For A Dead Dog': *Luna*

'I Am Writing This,' 'Oil,' 'Conch': *Main Street Rag*

'Elegy For Frank Zappa': *Seattle Review*

'Love,' 'State Of The Union': *Haight Ashbury Literary Review*

'Artifacts': *Portland Review*

'Fire': *Pacific Review*

'Landscape With A Row of Amputated Statues,' 'Jazz,'
    'Locomotion': *Ashville Poetry Review*

'Birthday,' 'The Carnival At The End Of The World'

    'Cells,' 'Clandestine Music': *International Poetry Review*

'Aubade': *The Kerf*

'That Year': *Poem*

'Bloodlines': *Southern Poetry Review*

'Deathwatch On The Potomac': *Painted Bride Quarterly*

A special thanks to
John Bradley, George Kalamaras, Robert Murphy
& Jane Eichwald
for making his book possible.

TABLE OF CONTENTS

—I—

—II—

—III—

—IV—

AMERICAN DUENDE

—I—

Black horses and sinister
people are riding
over the deep roads
of the guitar.

—Federico Garcia Lorca

An Introduction To The Alphabet

It is a country consumed by flames
And A is bludgeoned to death in an alley
B who must face a firing squad
Sits in his cell and writes long letters
C is a coward who hides in the trees
He is always exposed by the coming of winter
And D can no longer get out of bed
His fortunes rise in his dreams while his life disintegrates
And that butterfly tattoo on the buttock of E
The colors have faded now, the colors . . .

And F is a girl you knew   F
Like the dangling sex of a flower
G went to college and dropped out
The times were portentous
H grew a beard and emigrated to Canada
I joined the Merchant Marines
And the medical staff at several universities
Tried to recruit the recalcitrant   J
Who wanted nothing to do with foreign cadavers

And K painted pictures, pastoral scenes
In the last one you are gazing through the grin
of a broken window
L was struck by a car on a country road
And you remember the momentous occasion
When the last brick was laid after forty years
And M seemed to lean sideways like the cathedral
The fishermen went out anyway

It was up to N to bless the fleet
And in the great plaza of Taxco
You could hear a footstep echo for five hundred years

O disappeared in the night   twenty years old
O was last heard screaming for a medic
And the jungle took it all in
Meanwhile the hearts of the submarines froze
P stood his watch at two thousand fathoms
Q was pregnant
There was nothing to do with the mills shut down
And so we walked around for a long time
Not saying anything

R made it back from the war   R
109 pounds March 1972
Fell out of a loft and heard his hip
Break like a record album   they were playing the Rolling Stones
S woke up one night and left the house
He left his wife sleeping and his shoes
That were never destined to get very far
And T is in a mental institution in Vermont
He is totally organic now
The doctors chalk it up to bad LSD

U wanted to be filled with love
The last time I saw U alive
She was playing a flute and teaching English
To an Indian tribe in Guatemala
And V's construction business had gone bankrupt again
W lay on a beach in Costa Rica
We agreed that the disappearance of a few nuns
Didn't signify anything
and X rode his bicycle into the rain
He was last seen carrying watermelon

And Y stayed on with the CIA
He's in southern Spain now
Discussing ancient Roman sewer systems
With a drunken mandolin   the mandolin has information to sell
And Z spends a long time beside the shore
Z who could never get off his knees
The waves approach and fall back
With the rattle of a typewriter moving at tremendous speed . . .

The Silence Of The Aborigines

This might be west Texas
With its sparse scrub, dust
Swirling in the blast furnace of the wind.
The police have already shaken us down
For drugs, and let us leave Darwin
With a suspicious eye. This isn't a soil
Where pot can grow, my companion says,
Though we've come all the way from Hawaii
With seed enough to start a plantation.
He thinks he's Johnny Appleseed,
And we've already sown enough
To find a crop waiting in Samoa and New Guinea.

These Australians will drink to anything.
Towns are few and far between,
And then only a gas station-bar on the map.
They judge us Yanks by our clothes and boots,
And offer a toast to America,
Waiting for the next round to come their way
On us. *Last beer for 180 miles*
A sign might say,
And it's best to be prepared for anything.

I've heard Australians are the descendants
Of criminals sent over from England,
But it's best not to say so in public.
It's true, an old bush tells me.
We're invited to a party at the postmaster's house,
And the odor of singed water buffalo
Rises from a pit where a barbecue's in progress.
Chests of iced-down beer

Glimmer with the cold reality
That this night will end in a brawl,
And we'll both wind up in jail
Making license plates for the criminals.

No news from home is always good.
They don't ask for our draft cards here,
And we're on a mission.
A few soldiers on R&R from Vietnam
Try to dress like civilians,
And the one good looking waitress in town
Turns them down with a curt no thank you.
How many times has she been told
She's beautiful? A man weeps in his beer
Going back to the war,
And no one is happier than the bartender,
Who will sweep up the broken glass in the morning.

The Tunnel Rat
—For Paul

Here is your country: the dark
Gravity of rain, petals
Scattered to the wind,
And the voices of the dead far down the valley.
You will know the pandemonium of mosques,
The shuffling of lepers,
And the flight of the troubadours.
You will have seen the burned oxen,
Rats feasting from sacks of grain,
And the ears of enemies like dried apricots
Thrown down on a table.

You will know the appetite of fruit bats
And the notes Brazilian rosewood hides,
Purposes of dominion, anthrax,
Newspapers and predators,
Obituaries and eyeglasses.
Yes, and there are some things
you must keep to yourself:
How, in the forest one time . . .
The village going up in flames . . .

You must keep silent
About the torches and the unmarked graves,
Pacification, what napalm smells like
On a beautiful morning.
You must be careful
Not to use the word beautiful
Or everyone will think you're crazy,
You must be silent about the snakes
And what a pet mongoose can do
Going into an ambush.

You must say nothing of how it felt
To be alive, or what a .45
Sounds like in a tunnel.
You must forget the immolations,
The children with their severed arms,
How the beer in Saigon
Tasted slightly of embalming fluid,
The laughter of prostitutes,
Your job at the end of the day,
And crawling backwards from the anus of the world.

The Veteran

Your silence held a story
That could not find sound. Sometimes
A line would slip out as we rested
In the meager shade of a scrub oak
Gazing out across a valley: *Gooks*
Hated the mini-guns. A sentiment
Not profound, but proficient.
I think I, too, would dislike them,
And how they could plant a nail
In every square inch of a football field
In under sixty seconds.
When we worked, we worked hard,
Coiling the long cables about the yokes
Of our shoulders, stumbling
Up the talus slopes of hillsides
So bare no tree had taken root,
Each locked in his speculations
Of the American Dream.

Perhaps it was the helicopter
That took us off the mountain at dusk
That would set you off, its whirlwind
Chorus of arrival. Then pieces
Came out in a rush-how one man
In your squad kept a pet mongoose
That served as point on patrol.
The snakes he killed were skinned
And worn as hatbands. Your platoon
Was nicknamed *The Black Watch*
For its high body count.
The helicopter, an old Chinook,
Had signs in English and Vietnamese.
The pilot flew as if dodging bullets.
He laughed a lot, and was always drunk.

You never spoke of Georgia either,
Though your accent was thick, almost
Slurred to a drawl, and rural.
You could dodge the whirling blades
Better than anyone. Was it experience
That kept you alive those months
That dragged on forever? Your features
Seemed cut from native stone.
Once airborne, the words began again--
How another man carried a leather bag
Of severed human ears collected in combat
And how you saw him one night
Nibbling on one like a dried apricot
As you waited in ambush beside a trail
In the Mekong Delta.

Funeral Procession For A Dead Dog

The Doberman, dead for a week,
Lies where a bridge spans a dry canal
That marks the border of county and park.
No one is sure whose problem he is,
So management sends us with a truck
To get him out of sight and smell
Of the public. Seven days of summer heat
Have ripened him well.
We're glad we've brought our bandannas,
And bind them firmly over nose and mouth.

The corpse is stiff with rigor mortis
And weighs a ton. The tongue is curled
Between the teeth, as if he snarled
At the approaching car, and held his ground.
Magpies scold us from the nearby trees
For stealing a meal they think they've found.
He is harder to bag than the man
Who blew his brains out in a car
Parked above the reservoir.

The magpies follow us awhile,
A blind, black flock.
The shovels we brought to bury him
Rattle around in the back, and seem remote.
We could tie a rope around his neck
And take him for a drag on the beach
You say. *Or maybe we should put him*
In the ranger's car. And the thought
Of a dead dog propped behind the wheel
Of a thirty thousand dollar automobile
Makes us smile, and we both bark suddenly.

There's a pit downstream of the dam
Where the roadkill ends up, eventually.
How many corpses of deer
Have we dropped there already?

The tracks of mountain lions are everywhere.
It's a steep slope, almost sheer.
You lower the tailgate, while I
Make a judgement in the rearview mirror,
Gun the truck in reverse,
And brake just inches from the edge.
No one has thought to say a prayer.
The corpse tumbles out slowly into the gorge.

Landscape All Black

To begin with a black canvas
Is to find Federico alive,
Leaping over the minarets
In his cape of bats' wings
While the executioners stand
Terrified beside the road
That leads to a little olive grove
Where so many secrets are buried.
And to begin with so many secrets
Is to imagine the CIA,
Or the tiny flare of a match
On a street corner in Ft. Collins
When the moon doesn't rise
And the traffic on 1-25

Is backed up to Leningrad
Because of a blizzard,
And the amber lights
Of snowplows are churning a room
Where a pile of sheets on a bed
Resembles a woman dying of insomnia
And an owl shrieks *Jesus Christ*
Outside
In one of the dead cottonwoods.

To begin with a black canvas
Is to drive around all night
Gazing at Christmas lights
On houses so new no one
Has died in them yet,
Is to go out Baseline road
Considering suicide on the thin ice

Of the reservoir
Where a girl's face peers up
Through the black water at midnight,
And a passing gull strikes a power line,
Explodes for a moment into blue flame,
And a crow flies out of a field
Where a solitary gunshot

Cracks the stillness in a painting by Van Gogh
Who probably cooked
The subject of *The Pink Shrimps* in olive oil
And ate even the delicate shells
While the crow rested on a black branch
And looked at nothing like the eye of God.

That Year

When I decided not to kill myself
After the last failed affair,
I drove the back roads at night,
Watchful for the eyes of deer
Lurking beside fields stripped bare
In deep January. Once,
Rounding a curve, I hit
A six-point whitetail broadside
And flung him in a ditch.
I saw one antler shatter on the road.
He staggered slowly upright, wobbled
Like a newly born foal before
His eyes met mine, then bolted
Over a nearby fence, disappeared.
The year just begun was turning white.
I searched for blood trails in the snow
Until the wind drove me back.

That year my life unraveled like a tale
Told by a fool, I wandered the back roads
Searching for a one-horned deer
The night had gathered up,
And felt a kinship with his pain
That bore the scars of each aborted journey.
Why persist? The story's true:
I didn't kill myself. Most nights
I went to bed at dawn,
And so afraid of the dark
I left a light on, always.

Christmas

It's Christmas Eve
And I'm wondering why I'm still alive
There were so many women who wanted to kill me
There were so many bombs that didn't explode
Sometimes I could kiss my own loneliness
These days when I feel too lonely
I go down to the local mall
And mingle with the wandering herd
Who are all gazing intently into their smart phones
(I'm sure in the future human beings
Will be born with a smart phone
Instead of a left hand)
They glance up occasionally to see where they are
They are all searching for something that will make them happy
I too wander
Down hallways ablaze with lights
Where music flows like a chorus of angels
And because I want to get into the spirit of things
I search the crowd
For some revelation about the species
Or only a smile on a pretty face
I walk through the valley of my own shadow
And feel my loneliness slip away
As if I traveled under a starry sky
On the road to Bethlehem
And the cradle of that most famous dead man of all
                                    Jesus Christ.

—II—

Today the evil is clean
And prosperous, but it is
Everywhere, you don't have to
Take a streetcar to find it . . .
— Kenneth Rexroth

Meditation At Key West

Don't tell me there are no more dragons
Out there where the continent ends
At a solitary wharf slippery with blood,
Where a word leaving the mouth
Will freeze into vapor
And travel over the orange groves for a hundred miles
Before encountering a horse of fire.
And it is certain the rain
Won't wash the blood away,
And a shark will glide up the street
Suspended in the excessive melancholy of the air
That hangs in the footsteps of those
Who walk in pairs to perfumed dungeons
Where acid is served in paper cups
And a sad-eyed sailor stares from the balcony.

I will not speak of the oyster shells
Or of the women who die of insomnia.
I will not speak of the fish
Who surrender their armor to willing blades
So that their flesh can be eaten
By the light of a secretive lamp
Brought by a boy to his bed in a stable.
No. I am concerned with massive contusions.
I am concerned with the light that leaks
About the pallor of a face, with an earlobe
That resembles so many others.
I am concerned by an absence that is called Artaud.

Why does it rain? My shoes do not answer.
Is it possible I will meet a burning horse
That gallops over the pier of performers,
Scattering jugglers and mimes into terrified flight?
And should I cast an inquisitive glance
At the girl who carries the scars of a razor?
No. I am more curious about the dogs,
The dogs who only appear in black leather,
Who often howl the moon on its way
While the crowd outside of Sloppy Joe's
Stands there sedately under the rain.

But I have come to see the burning horse,
To glide with the sharks through the animal night,
To discourse with the grandsons of slaves
Who can't understand the meaning of the missing ear,
And to whom the name Artaud is a vegetable silence.
I have come to open the door to a room
Where death arrives dressed as a dark bandillero,
And I have come to inquire about the boy
Who falls asleep in the stable while reading Homer,
Who topples the lamp into the straw
And causes a horse to bolt into the road
Trailing the torch of a Castilian poncho.

Should I go now and eat a lobster?
Should I go down to the shore where the priests
Are defrocked, inquisitive, spreading the thighs of the moon?
No. I cower my animal half
Who would howl through the sleep of a fishing village,
Who would find both delight and fear
At the sight of a fire surrounding a horse
Whose hoofbeats are a telegram reaching a grave.

And remember the malignant honeybees,
The crazed herons looking like starved ambassadors,
The dragons that lumber from the wine-dark sea
And fill the night with chemical wonder,
Whose hungry roarings mingle with those
Of the last 29 Florida panthers
Who hurl themselves suicidally against the traffic
Out on highway 84.

The Owl

If he's still there, let him implicate
Some other poor poet to the crime
Of words. Night after night he perched
In the ragged elm outside my window
While I groped about for something to say
And found only pain and low wages.
His cry was singular, remote, his eyes
Like two lost moons that still revolved
About some extinct planet. I heard
The clock beside the bed tick down
And dreaded dawn, the oilfields,
Cursed the day about to begin
Before his cry could come again,
Relentless as a grand jury investigation.

Harvesters

They seem dull at first under the sweltering sun,
But have an edge to them: something in the eyes
That lift momentarily, the way a prisoner's eyes
Steal a look that takes everything in,
And then return to themselves.
If they feel anything at all, they're not letting on.

Even the young girls work.
They carry drinking water into the fields,
And it's certain that one of them
Has caught the eye of one of the young men.
They have the shyness of fireflies,
And something of the mystery in unwritten books.

The foremen curse the heat,
And count the crates of produce that are carried in.
They too have noticed the young girls,
And one of them has made a date
With the prettiest girl, who merely nodded.
The young men noticed. There will be blood.

It's the oldest story that there is.
One of the young men will kill the foreman
And be forced to flee for his own life.
But there is nowhere to go in a foreign country.

And in the camps at night
The old men will murmur of better times,
And the young girls will still carry water into the fields
As the days grow hotter.

The Plum

The beach is crowded today, so much flesh
Milling around, bodies pale after a long winter.
The lifeguards lounge in their chairs.
Their sunglasses reflect the light.
It's impossible to tell if their eyes are open.
One of them at least is still conscious.
She lifts a plum toward her mouth,
Stops, and admires it for a moment.
It's dark purple, like the hands
Of a man who has been in a fight,
Who returns to the orchards downcast, beaten.
He would like to have a girl like that,
A girl with brown legs that are always open
Like a fork in the trunk of a ripened tree.
Then a man could climb up and get at the fruit.
With a little luck, he could even make money.

In Memory Of The Citizens Of Colorado
Killed In The Vietnam War

This list of names never seems to end
On this plaque in the University
Memorial Center: Archuleta . . . Arnold . . .
They climb over themselves, become lost,
Disappear into dense foliage
Where it is raining.
Wind lashes against the windowpanes
This April day as I wait
For the reading to be over,
For the men in trenchcoats to come
And audit my taxes.
Perhaps I'm looking for a friend
Lost years ago: Jones . . . Jones . . . Jones
A boy with big arms who called me brother.
Nights we walked Denver's mean streets
Unafraid, and found what passed for an education.
Lives fly by in the wind.
Crabapple blossoms litter the street,
And students wander by, recently returned
From India, or Tibet.
The names go on,
I've tried counting them on my fingers
One by one, but they fall away, fade,
And I have to begin all over again:
Bates . . . Benitez . . . address unknown,
No rank or serial number,
A friend who might have been
The door-gunner on a Chinook,
The chopper going down in flames,

And the possibility that I might be
The only survivor
Rodriquez ...
Rodriquez ...
Rodriquez ...
Rodriquez ...
Rodriquez ...
Rodriquez ...
Rodriquez ...

Waltz

There are times when the darkness hesitates,
When a fragment of moonlight falls on the room
Like the glimmer of a knife, oily blue,
And even the drunks are suddenly silent.
There are times when words spoken softly have life,
And the smoke circulates,
Restless to be done with something.
The room is a sea full of staring, empty eyes,
And the few women present perk up:
It might be an interesting fight.
Now the combatants circle the floor.
It is like a dance you have seen performed
By one of those great, lanky cats in a cage,
The forefeet leading off with a slow
Steady rhythm that eats up time,
While the hindquarters follow at an adjusted distance.

Bloodlines

I am not immune, and in the world
Of lost loves, there are still a few
I cling to faithfully. An illiterate
Child for example, a porcelain
Face that winter shone through
Like a china doll's, and whose eyes
Were blue when she chose to open them.
For five days we stayed in bed
While the season grew long in the tooth
And the red-winged blackbirds deserted
The feeder. Father complained.
Fifteen going on thirteen, he said.
Mother, nearing a nervous breakdown again,
Cooked her way silently through the kitchen.

What thou lovest best, and Poe drinking
To kill the pain in a gutter. Others
Went underground on a dark day,
Or married, became religious fanatics
Who beat their children. And I can see her
Sometimes in my dreams, frustrated, worn out
With the work of keeping a household together.
Almost thirty now, her hair has lost
The silkiness that hangs from an ear of corn
When you strip it bare over a wastebasket.

Deathwatch On The Potomac

This is the slow work of piecing a life
Back together: insomnia in mental wards,
Dawns gazing out on falling snow, crows
Calling out from the cottonwoods
Like Lowell, anguished
Over a syllable, the blue shells
Of robins' eggs on the path
Where I often lose my way
Searching for an owl's feather,
Myths, the slow unraveling of things,
Love letters exhumed from steamer trunks
Where poems go to die, affairs as brief
As a match, or a moth
Drawn to a bowl of lamplit water.

These are the loose ends,
Threads of recovery I encounter each day,
Fields plowed under to conserve
What little soil remains
After a dry winter, the mummified
Corpse of a carp, or the paw
Some small creature left in a trap,
And Nixon dying of a stroke, I heard it
On the radio, and rushed home
To find this poem waiting, the man
Who declared he wouldn't be
The first American president to lose a war,
And had dogs loosed on the crowd
Gathered on the steps of the Capitol.
How have the years gone by?

I pick up a thread
And find blood on the face of a friend,
A thin boy who hitchhiked from Colorado
To hold another bleeding in his arms.
Cherry blossoms swirled in the street
Among the leavings of a light snow
That had recently fallen across the river.

—III—

It was for this that man came into the world, to fight
The serpent that advances in the whistle
Of things, in the glow
And the frenzy,
Like a glittering dust, to kiss
The bone of madness from within, to put
More and more love on the sheet
Of the hurricane, to write on his love act
The lightning of continued being, to play
This game of breathing in danger.

—Gonzalo Rojas

I Am Writing This

For Roque Dalton on a dark night
When certain pieces of moonlight fit
Inside the skull of a crow,
Writing it for the tarantulas
Who might know how much humanity exists
In a bottle of rum in the slums
Of Havana,
Writing it for Carlos Puig
Last seen on Megano Beach
Beside his makeshift raft
Waiting for fair weather,
Writing this because I must
For the fur-bearing seals and Australian pines,
Writing it for the Mississippi
Where I once saw a corpse
Rise up dragging chains,
Writing it for seagulls who burst into flames
Over the Arctic Circle,
Writing it for the whales and the ghosts
Who dance in the corn,
Writing it for Woody Guthrie's guitar
That says: *This machine kills fascists*,
That says to Roque:
Don't turn your back
On stagnant water,
That says to Carlos:
I'll come out for you
As far as Key West Light,
Writing this for the poem that creeps
Out of its envelope and crawls

Over the editor's desk
With thoughts of murder,
For my friends in prison,
For those who don't know what planet we're on,
And for the IRS, that would audit a corpse.

Elegy For Frank Zappa

Now the mudsharks reside in the bay
At Seattle, where America's lost children
Collect in an ecstasy of one-night stands,
And the guitars are raging
In the suburbs of Detroit,
In the backwoods of Tennessee,
On the reservations of North Dakota
Where a young Lakota chants
An elegy for the last wolf
Gunned down in Yellowstone,

And Los Lobos is playing border music
Below the hemisphere of airways,
And the ambulances are shrieking again
In East Los Angeles
Where the driver of a cigarette truck
Stops his rig, and stares
At three corpses the streets have washed up
And tells the kids closing in
Touch it, and I'll kill you,

And I too prefer music
That distributes razorblades to the poor,
The monosyllabics that come
From behind the screens in emergency wards
A music that comes out of Harlem,
From the South Side of Chicago,
A music that dies hard
On the streets of New Orleans at dawn
When the chain gangs are sweeping the garbage away
And someone begins: *Ain't no grave
Gonna keep my body down,*

And the end comes
Where the dream begins,
The guitars raging
Like the machine gun on a Chinook
Blazing obscenities down
On a little village
Where a child, looking up, sees God
Burst into flames, the pilot dead,
Slumped over the controls,
The dashboard clock still ticking.

Ode To Vladimir Mayakovsky

Vladimir Mayakovsky was a real live wire.
His verses after 2 AM
Glowed like candles in a cathedral,
And when he shouted obscenities
It could light up the Brooklyn Bridge.

Vladimir Mayakovsky was ten feet tall
And had a heart as big as a house.
Sometimes he would set the house on fire
And then leap out of himself.

Snowflakes are falling.
Wolves are loping over the Steppes.
Wolf, what happened at Tanguska?
Vladimir! Vladimir Mayakovsky!

Vladimir Mayakovsky was a prodigious lover,
But the woman he loved most of all was Russia.
How brightly he burned when he mounted a cloud
And just flew around in the darkness . . .

Love

Attila Jozsef, I love you,
Even though you're just some piece of flesh
Two people created one night
Because they were poor
And had no other outlet for their passion.
I love you because the moon rises,
And the satellite dish on the roof of a nearby house
Resembles a strange bird that has just flown in
All the way from Africa.
I love you even though your loneliness
Is like the shriek of a train
Before it enters an endless tunnel.
I love you because you are not Rilke
Or Pablo Neruda. I love you
Because you can't bake bread,
But never quit trying.
I love you because you don't take yourself
Too seriously. I love you because
You can still laugh at misfortune,
And even in these times
Aren't afraid of the government.
Attila Jozsef, you are a child of the universe.
You can spend all day studying a butterfly's wings
As if they were the Dead Sea Scrolls.
I love you because there are banyan trees in your poems
And wolves that leap with joy at falling snowflakes.
I know that Jesus is up in one of the banyan trees
                              And won't come down!

Music

Once
I was like the winged guitar
Of Ritchie Valens
(A little bit of Texas rattlesnake)
That was in the age of the turntables
It was in the age of UNICEF,
Radio Free Europe, and the atomic bomb
And first a dove flew out of the guitar
It was flying towards Mexico over the cotton fields

Flew over the river that gleamed
With chemical wonder
And it was Mardi Gras down below
Where flambeaus were dancing in the streets
And the music must have been jazz
That caused the constellation to spin
On the point of a needle
After all, it was in the age of the guitar
It was in the age of the death of the romantic
And astronauts were busy proclaiming
The deconstruction of the moon

And then a dragon leapt out of the guitar
It rose as smoke over the Mississippi Delta
A dragon with a thirst so great
It cast a giant shadow on the world
And the needles fell into their grooves
They fell into the arms of those
Who rode a saxophone into the night
And there was Hendrix on the airwaves
All the way from Honduras
Jerry Lee Lewis hammering the ivory bones
And the dragon roared
Incinerating the cotton fields

And the radios took it all in
They sent messages to the fishing boats
That had strayed far out on the black water
And the universe hummed in the strings
It said we might be nothing but notes
In the mind of God
And the planets were dancing to celestial music
Angels of crystal were flying over the roof
Strangers were knocking at the door
Begging shelter
The night was green with the beginning of love.

Artifacts

—for John Bradley

Not much remains, only
That sarape I bought in Taxco
Where you confessed the rings
From a short-lived marriage came from,
(I still wear it sometimes
When the wind is the coldest thing I can think of
Blowing through the broken windows of a train
Crossing Sonora), a night at Big Mike's
In Silver City, watching *Hud* on TV,
A huge brown trout from the Gila River
He kept embalmed in the freezer
And displayed proudly to anyone
Who would listen, a scarf
From Spain, more like a white flag
To be waved in the face of life
Those nights I struggled to write
A few good poems, and that coin
I had O'Haire drill a hole through
So I could wear it on a shoelace about my neck
To discourage those who always said
I'd die without a peso to my name.

Oil

It is what keeps the great machines
Running on time, what no army can go to war
Without, and Victor Serge starving in Mexico
Without a drop of oil to his name . . .
And it was in that time when the guitar
Had only five strings—taken out of its coffin
It would begin to play memories of the forest
Where it was born,
And because the guitar had only five strings
It was always searching for the lost note
Heard only by astronauts as they circled the globe,
And the globe was a blue lamp at the window
        Of space,
And it was oil that kept the light alive,
That kept the gears turning,
That kept the astronauts hurtling through space,
Oil that kept the tanks rolling through the desert,
And the guitar continued to play
Even though it had no oil,
It played for those returning from the war,
For those who stood on the picket-line
        Confronting the police,
It played for the lovers who would later be dust,
And for those who were sometimes found
Chained to machine guns in the forest,
And the astronauts gazed at the blue globe,
They saw Sydney, Australia, lit up like the moon,
They heard the hum of silence and praised oil
For bringing them this far,
After all, they were closer to God,
They were closer to the Sea of Tranquility,

And Victor Serge wandered through Mexico,
Sometimes he would climb onto the roof
Of the little boxcar he was riding in
And play the guitar that had only five strings,
The stars blazing overhead, as if someone
Rose up in the night like Van Gogh
And painted them . . .

Conch

A trumpet, to be blown on the cliffs
Of a grey coastline? A hollow, vibrant
Sound exists, and the listener, wanting more,
Might wear the puzzled look of one who holds
A telephone at the end of a long conversation.
Food for thought? A mollusk toughened,
Tasting of brine, that should be consumed
With the tender motions of an epicure
Dining alone in his room. And the shell,
Pink-hued where the tunnel unfolds . . .
How not to consider the wooden chair
Recently vacated by the exotic dancer
Who has left a small, luminous trail
A snail might leave, crossing an intimate plaza?

Fire

—for Pablo Neruda

Teacher I first read in the garden
Of the Hotel del Oro in San Miguel,
Instigator of a thousand small
Riots of flesh, pavilion behind which
The dancers undress, ceremony
Of earth and solitude, of light
That leaks beneath a kitchen door
Where the nostrils of the poor flare
At the odor of bread, love
That exists between men and women
Who face the same eternity together,
Worshiper of celery and thighs
Where the abyss gapes, bridgeless . . .

I remember a peacock in a cage,
And the empty basin of a fountain,
The flickering of votive candles
In shrines where miners tried and failed,
Where slavery answered the universal question,
And no one is left to redeem
The mummies in Guanajuato now.
I got sick, and almost died.
The cool porcelain where my forehead
Rested those nights comes to mind,
Somehow more soothing than the white
Touch of a woman.

Heart getting drunk on a flock of crows,
Furious beast on the floors of churches,
Electrical outlet for the intimate appeal,

Festival of the dying clocks,
Pylon rooted in the breath of time,
Harsh blue Andean sky
In which the last condor glides,
A crucifix above the looted temples,
Shark with the soft underbelly of light
Descending to the latitudes of the molecule . . .

Because, Pablo, that's what you are to me:
A torrential river that winds
Through the soul's vocabulary,
Fire that illuminates the sacred text
Of those who are forced to live on their knees,
Bright star that catches the eyes of lovers,
Mad flute played by someone up in a tree
Whose music alone keeps the heavens in motion.
I could mention other things.
Chile is no better off,
But workers are beginning to rise in Gdansk,
And American children
Are cutting sugarcane in Nicaragua.
How not to think of you
opening long furrows in the field,
Shouting down into the mouth of the mineshaft,
Commanding the terrified miners to rise up and walk.

Birthday

The clock keeps perfect time.
I know the way men go
When snow is falling, and it's late.
The snow keeps perfect time, the music waits
To trickle from our lives. Each death is slow,
And who can say what love is?
The lonely know. They often weep
From lack of poetry. Dreams
Are what a man does best,
Who has no plow.
He leaves no footprints in the snow
For wolves to follow.
He dreams an urchin in the street
Whose eyes are two live coals,
And remembers that scene from *The Seventh Seal*
Where the witch confesses nothing to lowly minds,
And Death is glimpsed briefly, dressed
As a clown, leading the newly deceased
Over a green hillside.
There are bundles of wheat in the background.
A white horse stands bewildered at the side of the road.

—IV—

People get ready,
there's a train a-comin',
you don't need no baggage,
you just get on board.

—*Curtis Mayfield*

The Platform

I am here on the platform, waiting
For the first vibrations of an approaching train
To rise through the soles of my feet
Like a music full of dark sounds,
Like a thunderstorm in which we feel ourselves caught,
And the music says: *whenever you see an abandoned shoe*
Think of me,
It is a poem by Cavafy that warns:
You will never escape the ruins of your life,
And I am here on the platform because
Here is where all journeys begin,
And what is music without dark sounds,
What is a poem without a train?

A train that hurtles on through the night
Past refrigerated glass towers where executives
Sign contracts, but know nothing about the dynamics
Of trains, past houses so new
No one has bothered to die in them yet,
Past autumn and the empty churches that stand
Like extinguished lamps, their congregations
Scattered to the four points of the wind,

A train that can hover in thin air
Like a great white shark, the locomotive
Stirring among the fossil beds of the Midwest,
An ancient intelligence, groping, secretive, blind,
The heartbeat of a drum along the shores
Of the Zambezi, a nomadic train
Steaming from jungle to jungle, gorged
On harvest, the great scythe-shaped fin
Parting the heavenly waters,

I mean the train that approaches like a judgement,
The train whose music is a flock of crows,
And I hope Casey Jones isn't at the throttle,
I hope the great white shark is asleep,

And it isn't a train, it's a guitar,
It isn't a platform, it's a launch pad,
And it's too late to disappear inside of a poem,
To paint the picture that begins with a drop of blood
And slowly fills the huge white canvas,
Because the train is already here,
And even my shadow is spreading its wings
To proclaim the final hour of the stars . . .

Landscape With A Row of Amputated Statues

At the end of the world we argued
While Dionysus sang, and Tesla
Converted the thunderbolt.
Someone was playing Hendrix offstage,
And Pythagoras was busy
Sketching out the parameters of the universe.
But who was building this landscape anyway?
Pyromaniacs invaded the paintings of Van Gogh.
At mid-afternoon the lioness licked her paws,
And a bull fell to its knees
Beside the carcass of a gored horse.
The shadow of the matador entered the room
Where three women were sewing a shroud for a journey,
And Dali danced on the stairway like Errol Flynn
Wielding his paintbrush like a sabre.
It was the hour of the opossum,
The year of the snake.
The moon bent over the weeping of guitars,
And herons drifted up from the marsh
Like the grey brush strokes of goodbye on a porcelain plate.

At the end of the world we argued.
Art is not for the sake of itself,
But should fill us someway
With its mysterious presence.
We agreed that the Earth was nothing more
Than a small speck of dust, and that perfect sonar
Existed in the salmon's skull.
Man is born without natural intelligence,
And lives by imitating what is.
In the secret chambers of himself

Einstein conceived of absolute zero
As the temperature at which atoms begin to flow
Into a new, undiscovered matter.
Summer came and disappeared. Autumn
Had no mercy on the insomnia of trains
Or ripped up lottery tickets. On the landscape of a potato
One man found God. Another
Raged about the proliferation of undocumented workers.

At the end of the world we argued.
Auden said: *If we saved*
Only those poems that survive with us
The test of time, the final outcome
Would be a volume so small no one would publish it.
He also asked if the whiskey came free
With the job of a poet laureate.
When the cats who stalk the pheasant-runs
Bristle at the dry thunders of July,
Anything can happen. *To deny magic*
Is to view sarcophagi for their ornateness.
Jellyfish popped like melons on the beach.
It was the twilight of the tarantula,
The season for serious storms.
When the paint had dried on the palates,
Thieves arrived at the houses of the poor
To steal the eyeglasses from the poets,
And snuff out the last candle in Arles.

Jim Morrison

Jim Morrison, you are a runaway train,
An angel of stone who stands guard
Over the black tolling of bells,
You are the bull on his knees in a circle of blood,
The bottomless note no one hears,
The cry that comes from the other side of God.
You are a field sown with dead crows.
It's impossible to talk to you.
You are the black cape that Lorca wore
When he soared over the rooftops of Grenada.

Yes. And you are also the final assault
Of butterflies, a lullaby for children
Who have fallen asleep in the snow.
You are a lost letter blown for a thousand miles,
And the last poem found in the pocket
   Of Attila Jozsef.
Attila Jozsef, the engineer muses.
Yes, I remember him,
But I never ran him down with my train.
He was always trying to burn down Budapest
All by himself, the crazy bastard.

Jazz

Here are the roads returning again
To a stable where you notice blood
On the straw, to the doorway of a brothel
Where a shadowy figure takes your hand
And the air has the scent of sweat and jasmine,
To nights spent walking beside the sea
Where the only light is the amber coal
Of a cigarette burned down to nothing,
To a cafe where artists collect,
Where you will often hear what Goebbels called
Nigger Kike jungle music,
To the distillation of words seeking their forms,
And the power of the mind to say nothing.

And there are no terminals, no dates
Fixed in the mind, nothing but *love*
To be uttered over a photograph
Of three teenagers with long hair,
And the landscape is Mexico
Or Vietnam, and the three are standing
In a jungle clearing, smiling, proud of themselves,
But the head in the middle has no body.
Who believes in the necessary good of man?
The roads return, the salmon swim
Upstream to die, and in every act
There's a small fragment of creation.

And here a pink parasol dissolves in the rain.
A whore leaves your side to feed
An infant with the breast she wanted
Five bucks more for you to touch,

Meanwhile the three teenagers
Are downstairs in the lounge,
They have finally found a rhythm
That seems acceptable to the crowd
Who want to dance, and spend their money
Jungle-fashion like this,

And there's nothing but *love* to be uttered
Over the harsh notes that sound
Like an M-16 on Rock n' Roll
To the man who wakes screaming,
Who understands now the nightmare is real,
And sometimes the disembodied head
Would have to rush outside
Where it was often found
Kneeling beside the gutter
Vomiting men, women, worlds.

Locomotion

Chaos is my country, land of disjointed things,
A self-portrait with electrical discharge,
And the body achieving locomotion again
For the man who says: *yes, I wrote poetry once,*
But I couldn't connect things, I couldn't
                    Connect . . .
And the huge angry eyes of the night
Shine on wheat fields that quiver with wind
In Saskatchewan, on runways where third-class mail
Crammed into duffel bags waits
For the last flight out or the Second Coming,
A body that dies of insomnia on the coast
Where a man walking a beach
Bends down to inspect a washed up shell
That reminds him of something vaguely human,
And the bright molecules of the neo-cortex
Light up a city that sleeps on its arms,
Or only a little cafe, where that madman, Tzara,
Is carving a dictionary into free speech . . .

Cells

The purpose of a cell
Is to destroy the enemy.
There are many cells on the road,
Gathering in a dark forest,
Preparing to invade a painting of Picasso's
Where an old guitarist slumps
In a tangle of strings and assassinated horses,
And the sea is moaning at the windows of shrines
Where books are beginning to give off light
Books that say the world breaks apart
Like the skeleton of a fish
When the weight of one footstep falls upon it,
And you won't know the battlefield
Even when you pass it at twilight,
Because someone has put the eyes
Of a dead iguana on a great man,
And the ice crystals of dawn
Bear the heavy thoughts of buffalo,
And the escalators are moving upstairs towards the stars.

Clandestine Music

Believe me,
There is so much suffering in the world
A soul can't contain it.
Electroshock helps, that
And swallowing a million goldfish.
Sometimes I feel like an aquarium: insane.
Once, I bit the head off of a crippled bird
For which act I got twenty years.
I was just hungry, that's all.
Do you know what it's like to dance with bears?
The music is good
When badgers creep out of their dens
To listen.

No, I never assaulted tourists with a 2x4
In Miami, and the rumor
That I'm secretly Poe on LSD
Is completely false.
If I fill you with dread
It's because you don't understand
How words can be written on the scorched wings of butterflies
After a fire has consumed the suburbs.
I understand these things.
I have universities in my blood.
I know worn out horses are led beneath the highway at dawn
To the local Purina factory.
I have heard their bones
Breaking before the furnaces are even lit.
I have an old harmonica
That says it's easier to cross over a bridge
With a handful of black widow spiders

Than the notes of a song about love,
That says hunger hurts like a kick in the balls,
And that it does no good
To threaten a cop with a lobster,
Or to scream: *Percodans! Give me Percodans!*
In the face of a startled priest.
I live in a hole beneath the earth
I call the tabernacle of the betrayed.
My friends are those who walk the high wire
Over the slums,
Wild men on the last train to Amsterdam,
The dead dog someone threw after Lowry into the ravine.

Aubade

There is a sadness in the eucalyptus trees
Because the butterflies do not return.
The mailboxes and pine coffins are empty
Because everyone has gone.
I leave for Burma at a bad time.
I cannot find myself in the streets of Grenada.
I was a bone's throw away from the emperor
When the assassins came.
I'll be lucky if I don't shoot myself in the ass.
I'll be lucky if I live to see tomorrow.
I have mocked the CIA,
And someone is thinking of me even now
As he stabs a table with an ice pick.
Susan, did you manage to save the whales?
I remember when you danced naked·
On the keel of the Shorewatcher's boat.
The house was dark, your hair
The russet color of a fox
Before he disappears into the underbrush.
I kept a quote by Bela Bartok
Above my bed: *Competitions are for horses,
Not artists.* I don't think I ever loved anyone,
Or perhaps I did and have forgotten it.
Memory is a spider's web
That's easily swept away
When the new owners arrive.
I'm sorry I had to burn the Van Gogh.
There were also a few gowns left in the attic
Among the mothballs and mice.
I pitied the mice.

They were so small
They could slip through the locks
Of the steamer trunks. I used to feed them
Slivers of cheese and the crumbs
Of Boston cream pie. I was only free
When I was in the forest,
But now the forest is gone,
And the butterflies do not return,
And I am only a poor carpenter
With nothing to say to the world except
Forgive me.

The Carnival At The End Of The World

And you will know by now that New Orleans
Was completely underwater
There were pianos floating by in the streets
There were small tribes of the saved
Clinging to rooftops
And the only way out was over the Huey P. Long bridge
And everybody knew that Huey P. Long
Was secretly a great white shark
He pulled many strings because he could
He could lick his own balls
He had more power than the President

And as I said the only way out was over the bridge
And it was really a steep climb
It was like crossing the Rocky Mountains
In a ghost train
And the city had run out of Dixie beer
It had run out of Jax and frozen daiquiris
And even the Romans knew
What can happen when the mob sobers up
And now that the mob was sober it was an ugly mob
It had already gutted the local Wallmart
It was torching the mansions of the rich
Down in the Garden District

And people were floating by in the streets
Clinging to pianos
There were great white sharks cruising around
But nobody could find Huey P. Long
And the river flowed on
It had come all the way from Minneapolis
Where no one in his right mind wants to be buried

And already the river had claimed many souls
They were seen dancing arm in arm
Just barely above the black water
And the mob was beginning to surge
To organize itself into a parade

And the great white sharks couldn't contain it
The mob was floating by clinging to pianos
To empty crates to the roofs of churches
And down by the river the chemical plants were on fire
They were like a thousand flambeaus dancing on the levee
And the streetcars were floating by
They were packed with survivors who waved
They resembled strange little steamships
Navigating their way down the Amazon
And the survivors waved but they had no faces
Someone was beating a drum on the shore
And the city by torchlight resembled a tomb
The dead were beginning to rise from their coffins . . .

ABOUT THE AUTHOR

JAY GRISWOLD was born in New Orleans, Louisiana, and has traveled extensively throughout the world. He has a Masters Degree in Creative Writing from Colorado State University and currently resides in Ft. Myers, Florida. His previous books are *Meditations for the Year of the Horse* (Leaping Mountain Press) and *The Landscape of Exile* (West End Press, 1993)

For the full Dos Madres Press catalog:
www.dosmadres.com